Sports Illustrated KIDS

STATS!

The GREATEST NUMBERS in Sports

Managing Editor, SPORTS ILLUSTRATED KIDS **Bob Der**

Creative Director **Beth Bugler**

Project Editor **Andrea Woo**

Director of Photography **Marguerite Schropp Lucarelli**

Photo Editor **Annmarie Avila**

Writer **Justin Tejada**

Copy Editor **Megan Collins**

Designer **Kirsten Sorton**

Reporter **Ryan Hatch**

Imaging **Geoffrey Michaud, Dan Larkin**

TIME HOME ENTERTAINMENT
Publisher: Jim Childs
Vice President, Brand & Digital Strategy: Steven Sandonato
Executive Director, Marketing Services: Carol Pittard
Executive Director, Retail & Special Sales: Tom Mifsud
Executive Publishing Director: Joy Butts
Director, Bookazine Development & Marketing: Laura Adam
Finance Director: Glenn Buonocore
Associate Publishing Director: Megan Pearlman
Assistant General Counsel: Helen Wan
Assistant Director, Special Sales: Ilene Schreider
Senior Book Production Manager: Susan Chodakiewicz
Design & Prepress Manager: Anne-Michelle Gallero
Brand Manager: Jonathan White
Associate Prepress Manager: Alex Voznesenskiy
Assistant Brand Manager: Stephanie Braga

Editorial Director: Stephen Koepp

Special thanks: Katherine Barnet, Jeremy Biloon, Rose Cirrincione, Jacqueline Fitzgerald, Christine Font, Jenna Goldberg, Hillary Hirsch, David Kahn, Amy Mangus, Kimberly Marshall, Amy Migliaccio, Nina Mistry, Dave Rozzelle, Ricardo Santiago, Adriana Tierno, Vanessa Wu

9

AP NATIONAL CHAMPIONSHIPS

won by **Alabama**. The Crimson Tide was tied with Notre Dame going into the 2012 season but grabbed the edge when it defeated the Irish 42–14 in that season's BCS national title game.

IN A FLASH Usain Bolt of Jamaica retained the title of world's fastest man when he broke his own 100-meter record with a time of 9.58 seconds.

CONTENTS

56 CONSECUTIVE GAME

7 NO-HITTERS

15,806 CAREER ASSISTS

5,714 CAREER STRIKEOUTS

21 CONSECUTIVE GAMES

Unbreakab

8 SEASONS

2,632 CONSECUTIVE GAMES

56 POINTS

4

2,857 POINTS

714 CAREER HOME RUNS

MVP AWARDS

4

NFL MVP AWARDS won by **Peyton Manning**. He is the only four-time winner of the award. Manning, who spent 14 seasons with the Indianapolis Colts before joining the Denver Broncos in 2012, was league MVP in back-to-back seasons twice: He received the honor in 2003, '04, '08, and '09.

POINTS scored by center **Wilt Chamberlain** of the Philadelphia Warriors in a game against the New York Knicks on March 2, 1962. Chamberlain's prolific output led the Warriors to a 169–147 win. He finished the season averaging 50.4 points per game, an NBA record.

CONSECUTIVE GAMES in which Joe DiMaggio of the New York Yankees had a hit in 1941. DiMaggio hit a single against the Chicago White Sox on May 15, 1941, and hit safely in every game the Yankees played through July 16. He had a total of 91 hits in 223 at bats during the streak for a .408 batting average. Joltin' Joe went on to lead the Yankees to a World Series title that season and was named the American League MVP.

22,895

CAREER RECEIVING YARDS by **Jerry Rice** during his 20 NFL seasons, a league record. The mark is just one of Rice's many accomplishments. He also holds the all-time NFL records for receptions (1,549) and touchdowns (208).

WAYNE GRETZKY: His Numbers

2,857

POINTS that Gretzky scored in his career, the most ever. He also holds the all-time records for goals (894) and assists (1,963).

4

STANLEY CUPS that Gretzky won with the Edmonton Oilers. He also led the Los Angeles Kings to the Cup finals in 1992–93.

40

REGULAR-SEASON RECORDS that Gretzky held at the time of his retirement in 1999.

6

YEARS OLD, Gretzky's age when his father, Walter, built an ice rink in the family's backyard.

39

GAMES that it took Gretzky to score 50 goals in 1981–82. No other NHL player has reached the 50-goal plateau faster. He finished the season with a single-season-record 92 goals.

99

GRETZKY'S JERSEY NUMBER, which was retired league-wide by the NHL in 2000.

378

GOALS that Gretzky scored in one season as a peewee in his hometown of Brantford, Ontario, Canada.

9

TIMES that Gretzky won the Hart Trophy as the NHL's most valuable player.

15,806

CAREER ASSISTS by **John Stockton**, an NBA record. Stockton played all 19 of his seasons in the league with the Utah Jazz and helped the team reach the playoffs in all of those seasons. He led the NBA in assists for nine consecutive seasons.

511

CAREER WINS by Cy Young. The righthander won 30 games in a season five times and exceeded 20 wins in 15 seasons. Included in his wins is a perfect game on May 5, 1904. For someone to get anywhere close to Young's mark, he would have to win 25 games for 20 seasons. In an era when few pitchers reach even 20 wins in a season, Young's record seems secure.

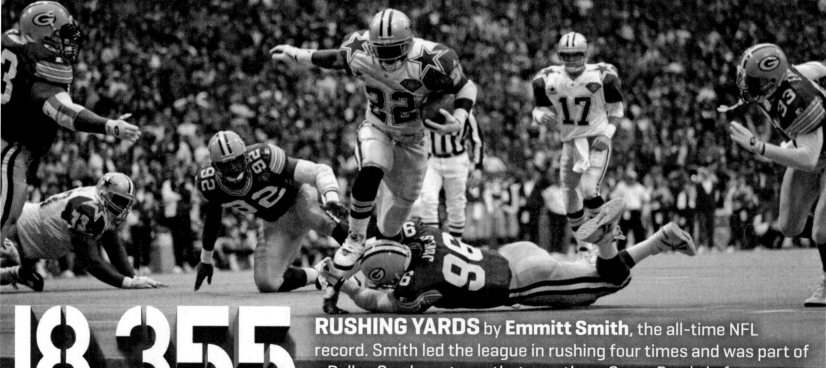

18,355

RUSHING YARDS by **Emmitt Smith**, the all-time NFL record. Smith led the league in rushing four times and was part of a Dallas Cowboys team that won three Super Bowls in four years. Smith also holds the record for most rushing touchdowns (164) and most 100-yard rushing games (78).

139

POINTS scored by the Boston Bruins' **Bobby Orr** in 1970–71, the most by an NHL defenseman in a single season. That season Orr won the Hart Trophy as league MVP and the Norris Trophy as the NHL's top defenseman. He finished his career with three MVP awards and eight Norris Trophies.

167

SINGLES TITLES won by Martina Navratilova during her career, a record. Eighteen of Navratilova's championships were in Grand Slam events, including nine at Wimbledon. She was equally skilled playing doubles. She has 177 career doubles titles, another record, with 31 of them coming at Grand Slams.

Winning Ways

103

CONSECUTIVE GAMES without a loss by the **University of North Carolina** women's soccer team from September 30, 1986, to September 17, 1990. The Tar Heels won 97 games and four national titles over that span.

21 CONSECUTIVE GAMES, including the playoffs, that the **New England Patriots** won from October 2003 through October 2004. The Patriots' streak included a victory over the Carolina Panthers in Super Bowl XXXVIII. New England also had a perfect regular season in 2007 but lost to the New York Giants in the Super Bowl.

151

CONSECUTIVE HIGH SCHOOL FOOTBALL WINS by De La Salle High School. The Concord, California, school's streak ended in 2004 after 12 perfect seasons. Jacksonville Jaguars running back Maurice Jones-Drew, a De La Salle alum, never lost a game in high school.

11

CONSECUTIVE TOURNAMENT VICTORIES by Byron Nelson in 1945. Nelson's run included winning the PGA Championship. He finished the season with 18 titles, also a record.

112

CONSECUTIVE MATCHES that beach volleyball players Misty May-Treanor and Kerri Walsh Jennings won from August 19, 2007, to August 31, 2008.

98

CONSECUTIVE MATCHES that tennis player Bill Tilden won between 1924 and '25, the longest streak in men's tennis. Tilden also won six consecutive United States singles championships, from 1920 to '25.

47

CONSECUTIVE NCAA DIVISION 1A FOOTBALL VICTORIES by the Oklahoma Sooners. Oklahoma's run stretched from October 10, 1953, through November 9, 1957, with the team amassing 12 wins more than its closest competitor. During the streak, the Sooners won two national championships and had three undefeated seasons.

76

GOALS that Teemu Selanne scored as a rookie in 1992–93. The Winnipeg Jets right wing blew the previous record of 53 goals out of the water. Selanne hit the back of the net 11 times in his first 12 games and never let up. At age 42, Selanne is still an offensive threat for the Anaheim Ducks.

14

CONSECUTIVE GAMES
that Detroit Lions running back **Barry Sanders** rushed for more than 100 yards in 1997, an NFL record. Sanders started the season slowly, with just 53 total rushing yards in his first two games, but then he caught fire and passed the 100-yard mark in every game for the rest of the regular season. His streak also included two games in which he rushed for more than 200 yards. He finished the season with a league-leading 2,053 yards.

IRONMEN OF SPORTS

964

CONSECUTIVE GAMES played by Doug Jarvis. The NHL center played in his first game on October 8, 1975, and did not miss a regular season contest until he retired 13 seasons later. Over the course of his career, Jarvis played for the Montreal Canadiens, Washington Capitals, and Hartford Whalers.

297

CONSECUTIVE GAMES started by quarterback Brett Favre. His streak spanned 19 seasons, with the Green Bay Packers, New York Jets, and Minnesota Vikings. During that stretch, Favre became the NFL's all-time leader in completions, passing touchdowns, and passing yards.

2,632

CONSECUTIVE GAMES played by Cal Ripken Jr. The Baltimore Orioles star was in the lineup for every game from May 30, 1982, through September 19, 1998. Ripken eclipsed the record of 2,130 that had been set by New York Yankees great Lou Gehrig. Ripken was a 19-time All-Star who won two American League MVPs.

1,192

CONSECUTIVE GAMES played by A.C. Green. It's no surprise that Green's Twitter handle is @NBA_Ironman. From November 19, 1986, through April 18, 2001, Green suited up for every game. Along the way he won three NBA championships and played for the Los Angeles Lakers, Phoenix Suns, Dallas Mavericks, and Miami Heat.

7

NO-HITTERS thrown by **Nolan Ryan**. No other pitcher has thrown more than four. Ryan tossed his first no-no when he was 26 years old and his last when he was 44. Four of his no-hitters came with the California Angels, one with the Houston Astros, and two with the Texas Rangers. As impressive as Ryan's seven no-hitters are, he came close to having even more. He had 24 no-hitters broken up in the seventh inning or later.

5,714

CAREER STRIKEOUTS by **Nolan Ryan**. With his 100-mile-per-hour fastball, the righthander was a dominating presence on the mound. His strikeout total is 839 more than his closest competitor.

30.8, 12.5, 11.4

AVERAGE POINTS, REBOUNDS, AND ASSISTS, respectively, by Cincinnati Royals point guard Oscar Robertson in 1961–62. He is the only NBA player to average a triple double for an entire season. When Robertson retired, he was the highest-scoring guard of all time and had the most career assists.

Babe

60
HOME RUNS
that Ruth hit in 1927, setting a single-season record that stood for 34 years.

7
WORLD SERIES– WINNING TEAMS
that Ruth was a part of. He won three times with the Boston Red Sox and four with the New York Yankees.

Ruth: His Numbers

714

CAREER HOME RUNS that Ruth had hit when he retired after the 1935 season. No player had ever hit more at the time, and Ruth's career record stood until Hank Aaron broke it in 1974.

1920

YEAR that Ruth was sold from the Red Sox to the Yankees. This started what became known as the Curse of the Bambino. Boston had five World Series titles before dealing Ruth, but did not win another one until 2004.

89

GAMES that Ruth won as a pitcher with the Red Sox. Though known more for his offense, Ruth was an impressive hurler who led the American League in ERA in 1916.

4,256

CAREER HITS by **Pete Rose**, making him baseball's all-time hit king. During Rose's 24 seasons in the big leagues, he won three batting titles and finished 10 seasons with 200 or more hits.

8

SEASONS that Jim Brown led the NFL in rushing. The Cleveland Browns running back led the league during his Rookie of the Year season in 1957 and then proceeded to repeat the feat in seven more of the nine seasons he played in the NFL. Brown won three AP MVP awards and was elected into the Hall of Fame in 1971.

56

POINTS that **Lew Alcindor** scored in his first varsity game for UCLA, against USC on December 3, 1966, an all-time high for a first game. Alcindor, who later changed his name to Kareem Abdul-Jabbar, was so dominant that the NCAA banned dunks as a way of slowing down his offense. Alcindor won an NCAA championship in each of his three seasons on UCLA's varsity team.

54

CONSECUTIVE GAMES

in which New Orleans Saints quarterback **Drew Brees** completed a touchdown pass. Brees broke the NFL record in Week 5 of the 2012 season. The mark had been previously held since 1960 by Baltimore Colts quarterback Johnny Unitas, who had 47 consecutive games with a TD pass.

3,830

CAREER BLOCKS by center Hakeem Olajuwon, an NBA record. During Hakeem the Dream's 18 seasons with the Houston Rockets and Toronto Raptors, he led the league in blocks per game three times and was twice named Defensive Player of the Year. Olajuwon's defense helped lead the Rockets to back-to-back NBA titles in 1993–94 and '94–95.

10

CONSECUTIVE SEASONS with at least 200 hits by **Ichiro Suzuki**. Ichiro had played nine seasons in Japan before joining the Seattle Mariners in 2001, and his experience paid off. He had 242 hits as a rookie, and topped the 200-hit plateau in each of the next nine seasons, leading the American League in the category seven times. The only other player with 10 200-hit seasons is Pete Rose, but he accomplished the feat over a span of 15 seasons.

91

GOALS scored by **Lionel Messi** for FC Barcelona and Argentina in 2012. Messi set the record for the most scores in a calendar year, topping the previous mark of 85 that had been set by Gerd Müller in 1972.

1,281

GOALS scored by Pelé in his career, the most ever. The Brazilian soccer great had 92 hat tricks and won three World Cup titles. In one club game in 1964, Pelé had a whopping eight goals.

ALFONSO SORIANO
Outfielder, Washington Nationals

Year: 2006
46 home runs, 41 stolen bases

ALEX RODRIGUEZ
Shortstop, Seattle Mariners

Year: 1998
42 home runs, 46 stolen bases

BARRY BONDS
Outfielder, San Francisco Giants

Year: 1996
42 home runs, 40 stolen bases

JOSE CANSECO
Outfielder, Oakland A's

Year: 1988
42 home runs, 40 stolen bases

4

PLAYERS

in major league history who have hit at least 40 home runs and stolen at least 40 bases in a season. Here are the members of the exclusive 40-40 club.

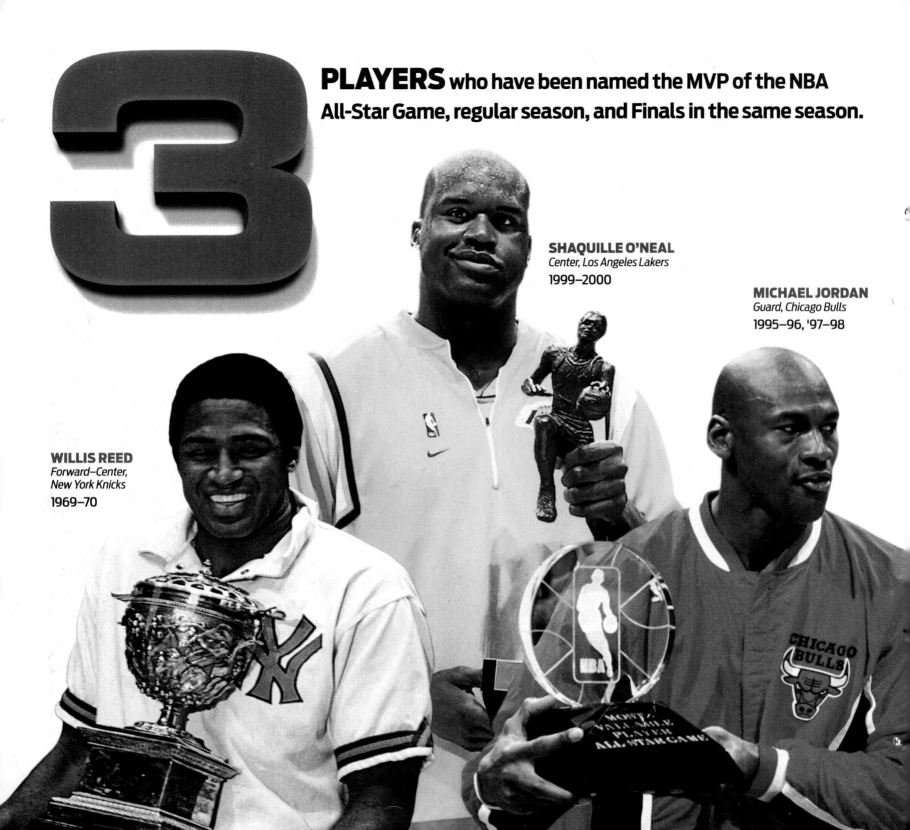

3

PLAYERS who have been named the MVP of the NBA All-Star Game, regular season, and Finals in the same season.

SHAQUILLE O'NEAL
Center, Los Angeles Lakers
1999–2000

MICHAEL JORDAN
Guard, Chicago Bulls
1995–96, '97–98

WILLIS REED
Forward–Center,
New York Knicks
1969–70

23

TOUCHDOWN RECEPTIONS

by **Randy Moss** of the New England Patriots in 2007. Moss broke Jerry Rice's NFL single-season record for TDs in his first season with the Pats and also set the franchise record for receiving yards (1,493). Moss had a touchdown grab in all but three of New England's games in '07 and racked up four against the Buffalo Bills on November 18.

COURT No. 18

Nicolas MAHUT · 2 68 30

John ISNER · 2 69 40

11 HOURS 5 MINUTES

LENGTH of the tennis match between **John Isner** and Nicolas Mahut during the first round of Wimbledon in 2010. It is the longest tennis match in history and took place over three days. Each player served more than 100 aces. Isner finally emerged triumphant by a score of 6–4, 3–6, 6–7 (7–9), 7–6 (7–3), 70–68.

12

THREE-POINTERS

that Los Angeles Lakers guard **Kobe Bryant** sunk in a game against the Seattle SuperSonics on January 7, 2003. His hot streak from behind the arc included nine threes in a row, an NBA record. Before the game against the Sonics, Bryant's previous high for 3-pointers made was five. Two years later, Donyell Marshall of the Toronto Raptors tied Bryant's record in a game against the Philadelphia 76ers.

63

YARDS, length of the longest field goal made in NFL history. Four kickers have booted it between the uprights from that distance.

TOM DEMPSEY, *New Orleans Saints* (1970)
JASON ELAM, *Denver Broncos* (1998)
SEBASTIAN JANIKOWSKI, *Oakland Raiders* (2011)
◄ **DAVID AKERS,** *San Francisco 49ers* (2012)

19

SEASONS that **Steve Yzerman** was the captain of the Detroit Red Wings. No other NHL player has worn the "C" on his jersey longer. The center played his entire career with the Wings. He was named the team's captain prior to the 1986–87 season (his fourth with the club) and served in that capacity until he retired in 2005–06.

11

ASP WORLD CHAMPIONSHIP TITLES that surfer **Kelly Slater** has won. In 1992, at the age of 20, Slater became the youngest person to win the title in just his second year on tour. In 2011, he became the oldest at age 39. Slater's title run may not be over. He finished second in 2012, and the title chase came down to the final event of the season.

23

MLB PITCHERS
who have thrown a perfect game.

LEE RICHMOND, *Worcester Ruby Legs*	June 12, 1880
MONTE WARD, *Providence Grays*	June 17, 1880
CY YOUNG, *Boston Pilgrims*	May 5, 1904
ADDIE JOSS, *Cleveland Naps*	October 2, 1908
CHARLIE ROBERTSON, *Chicago White Sox*	April 30, 1922
DON LARSEN, *New York Yankees*	October 8, 1956
JIM BUNNING, *Philadelphia Phillies*	June 21, 1964
SANDY KOUFAX, *Los Angeles Dodgers*	September 9, 1965
CATFISH HUNTER, *Oakland A's*	May 8, 1968
LEN BARKER, *Cleveland Indians*	May 15, 1981
MIKE WITT, *California Angels*	September 30, 1984
TOM BROWNING, *Cincinnati Reds*	September 16, 1988
DENNIS MARTINEZ, *Montreal Expos*	July 28, 1991
KENNY ROGERS, *Texas Rangers*	July 28, 1994
DAVID WELLS, *New York Yankees*	May 17, 1988
DAVID CONE, *New York Yankees*	July 18, 1999
RANDY JOHNSON, *Arizona Diamondbacks*	May 18, 2004
MARK BUEHRLE, *Chicago White Sox*	July 23, 2009
DALLAS BRADEN, *Oakland A's*	May 9, 2010
ROY HALLADAY, *Philadelphia Phillies*	May 29, 2010
PHILIP HUMBER, *Chicago White Sox*	April 21, 2012
MATT CAIN, *San Francisco Giants*	June 13, 2012
FELIX HERNANDEZ, *Seattle Mariners*	August 15, 2012

CROWNING ACHIEVEMENT
In 2012, King Felix shut out the Tampa Bay Rays 1–0 to record the 23rd perfect game in major league history.

33

STRAIGHT VICTORIES

that the Los Angeles Lakers reeled off during the 1971–72 season. The Lakers lost on Halloween night, October 31, 1971, and did not drop another game until January 9, 1972. The team featured stars like guard **Jerry West**, forward Elgin Baylor, and center Wilt Chamberlain. The Lakers finished the season 69–13, then cruised through the playoffs and defeated the New York Knicks in the NBA Finals.

40

POINTS scored by the Chicago Cardinals' **Ernie Nevers** in a game against the Chicago Bears on November 28, 1929. Nevers rushed for six touchdowns, and also kicked four extra points. His mark is the oldest NFL record. Nevers, who is in the pro and college football Halls of Fame, was also a reliever for the St. Louis Browns.

2

MAJOR LEAGUERS

who have won the Rookie of the Year and MVP awards in the same season. Centerfielder **Fred Lynn** of the Boston Red Sox did it in 1975, when he led the American League in runs, slugging percentage, and on-base percentage to help Boston win the AL pennant. No one repeated the feat until 2001, when the Seattle Mariners' Ichiro Suzuki pulled it off. That season Ichiro led the AL in batting average, steals, and hits.

16 SEEDS that have defeated a Number 1 seed in the NCAA men's basketball tournament. A 15 seed has beaten a 2 seed seven times in NCAA history, including Florida Gulf Coast, which upset Number 2 Georgetown in 2013. The underdog Eagles went on to become the first 15 seed to reach the Sweet 16.

.406

BATTING AVERAGE of Boston Red Sox leftfielder **Ted Williams** in 1941. Williams was the last major leaguer to hit over .400, a mark which has been reached 27 times in big league history. Since '41, only two players have topped .390: George Brett of the Kansas City Royals (.390 in 1980) and Tony Gwynn of the San Diego Padres (.394 in 1994).

THE .400 CLUB

Besides Ted Williams, only seven other modern-era players have maintained a .400 average to end the season. Here are the other 20th-century major leaguers who reached the mark.

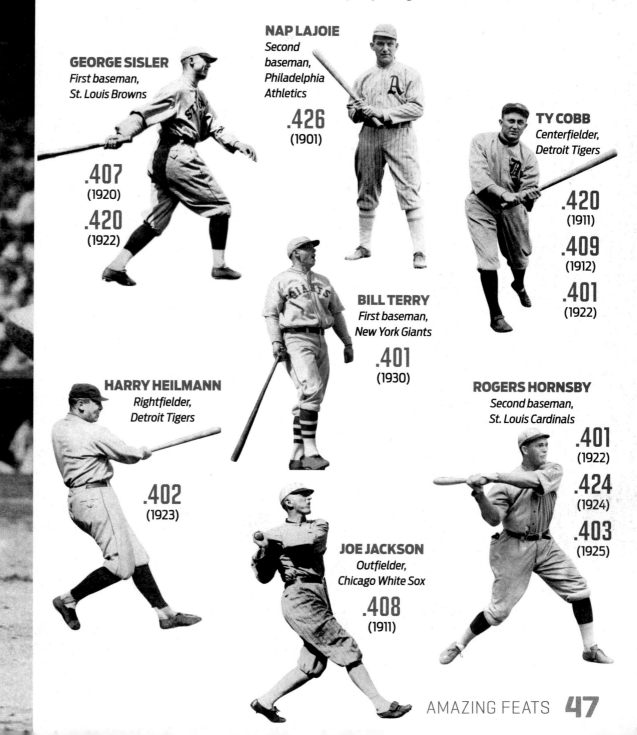

NAP LAJOIE
Second baseman, Philadelphia Athletics

.426
(1901)

GEORGE SISLER
First baseman, St. Louis Browns

.407
(1920)

.420
(1922)

TY COBB
Centerfielder, Detroit Tigers

.420
(1911)

.409
(1912)

.401
(1922)

BILL TERRY
First baseman, New York Giants

.401
(1930)

HARRY HEILMANN
Rightfielder, Detroit Tigers

.402
(1923)

ROGERS HORNSBY
Second baseman, St. Louis Cardinals

.401
(1922)

.424
(1924)

.403
(1925)

JOE JACKSON
Outfielder, Chicago White Sox

.408
(1911)

104.9

CAREER PASSER RATING for quarterback **Aaron Rodgers** of the Green Bay Packers through the 2012 season. Rodgers is the all-time leader in passer rating. (No other QB has a career rating higher than 100.) The Packers signal-caller also set the single-season record for passer rating in 2011 (122.5). The highest possible passer rating a player can have in the NFL is 158.3.

75 FEET, length of the pass that Duke's Grant Hill heaved toward teammate **Christian Laettner** in the 1992 NCAA tournament East region final. Duke trailed Kentucky 103–102 in overtime with 2.1 seconds left in the game. Laettner caught the ball near the free-throw line and made a turnaround fadeaway jumper as time ran out to give the Blue Devils the win. The win propelled Duke to the Final Four, and the team went on to win its second consecutive national championship.

10

CONSECUTIVE BATTERS that New York Mets pitcher **Tom Seaver** struck out in a game against the San Diego Padres on April 22, 1970. His first K of the streak came with the last out in the bottom of the sixth inning. Seaver then struck out the side for each of the next three innings. He finished with 19 strikeouts and allowed only two hits in the 2–1 complete-game victory.

33

CONSECUTIVE WEEKS that the USC Trojans were ranked Number 1 in the AP Poll, from December 8, 2003, through December 4, 2005. While sitting atop the rankings, the Trojans, led by quarterback **Matt Leinart**, won two AP national championships. (USC was stripped of its 2004 BCS national title due to NCAA violations.)

12

STROKES, margin of victory for **Tiger Woods** when he won his first major tournament, the 1997 Masters. At age 21, Woods became the youngest Masters champion and set the record for the largest margin of victory at Augusta. He would go on to set margin-of-victory records at two other majors, the U.S. Open and the British Open.

200

CAREER NASCAR WINS by **Richard Petty**, the most ever. Nicknamed the King, Petty ruled the track. He won 27 races in 1967 and was a seven-time Daytona 500 champion. Petty comes from a family of race-car drivers. His father, Lee, won the first Daytona 500, and his son, Kyle, competed in more than 800 NASCAR Sprint Cup races.

DAYTO

90

CONSECUTIVE WINS by the UConn women's basketball team, the longest streak in men's or women's college basketball. The Huskies' streak began on November 16, 2008, with an 82–71 win over Georgia Tech. It did not end until December 31, 2010. In between, UConn won two national championships and trailed for only 134 out of the total 3,600 minutes that it played.

406

RUSHING YARDS by TCU running back LaDainian Tomlinson against UTEP on November 20, 1999. Tomlinson became the first rusher in Division I-A history to break the 400-yard barrier. He also scored six TDs in the 52–24 victory.

730

PASSING YARDS by Old Dominion's Taylor Heinicke in a game against New Hampshire on September 22, 2012. Heinicke set the Division I record by completing 55 of 79 passes for five touchdowns, leading his team to a 64–61 win. The previous mark was held by Houston's David Klingler, who threw for 716 yards against Arizona State in 1990.

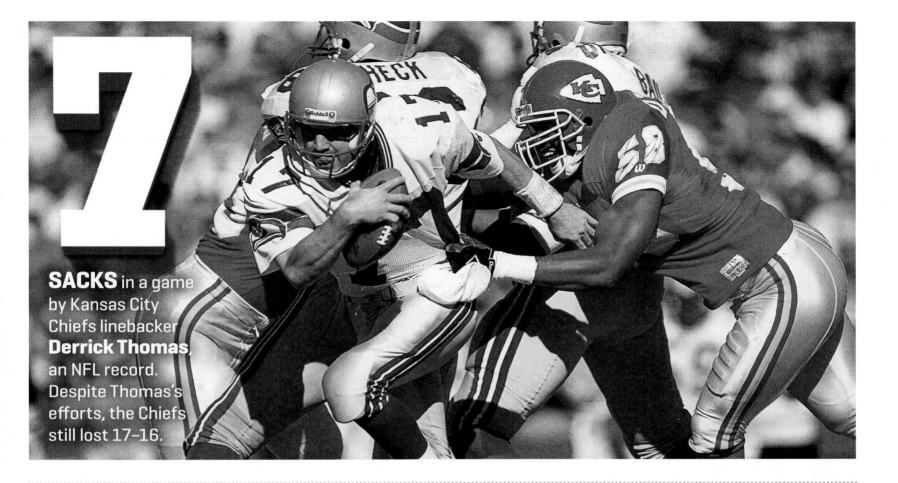

7

SACKS in a game by Kansas City Chiefs linebacker **Derrick Thomas**, an NFL record. Despite Thomas's efforts, the Chiefs still lost 17–16.

.981

FREE-THROW PERCENTAGE of guard **Jose Calderon** of the Toronto Raptors in 2008–09, an NBA single-season record. Calderon missed only three of his 154 free-throw attempts during the season.

24

PITCHERS who have won at least 300 games in the major leagues. The last player to do so was Randy Johnson in 2009.

CY YOUNG, 511
WALTER JOHNSON, 417
PETE ALEXANDER, 373
CHRISTY MATHEWSON, 373
PUD GALVIN, 365
WARREN SPAHN, 363
KID NICHOLS, 361
GREG MADDUX, 355
ROGER CLEMENS, 354
TIM KEEFE, 342
STEVE CARLTON, 329
JOHN CLARKSON, 328

EDDIE PLANK, 326
NOLAN RYAN, 324
DON SUTTON, 324
PHIL NIEKRO, 318
GAYLORD PERRY, 314
TOM SEAVER, 311
OLD HOSS RADBOURN, 309
MICKEY WELCH, 307
TOM GLAVINE, 305
RANDY JOHNSON, 303
LEFTY GROVE, 300
EARLY WYNN, 300

14

INTERCEPTIONS that cornerback Dick "Night Train" Lane of the Los Angeles Rams had in 1952, his rookie season. Lane had joined the Rams after four years in the Army and made an immediate impact on defense. He ran two of the picks back for touchdowns. Lane was elected to the Pro Football Hall of Fame in 1974.

48

YARDS, length of the Hail Mary pass that Boston College quarterback **Doug Flutie** completed to receiver Gerard Phelan for a touchdown on November 23, 1984. Flutie's pass came as time was running out and gave the Eagles a 47–45 victory in the matchup between two of the country's top teams.

608

SAVES by **Mariano Rivera** of the New York Yankees through the 2012 season. Rivera became the all-time leader in saves thanks to his cut fastball, which baffles lefthanded and righthanded hitters alike. He has been especially dominant in the postseason, where he holds the all-time record for lowest ERA (0.70) and has helped the Yankees win five World Series.

2

20

YEARS OLD, age of Texas A&M quarterback **Johnny Manziel** when he won the Heisman Trophy in 2012, becoming the first freshman ever to win the award. Nicknamed Johnny Football, Manziel passed for 3,760 yards and ran for 1,410 more on a Texas A&M team that ranked fifth in the season-ending AP poll.

HEISMAN TROPHIES won by running back **Archie Griffin** of Ohio State. Griffin is the only two-time winner of college football's most prestigious trophy. As a junior in 1974 he rushed for 1,695 yards and 12 touchdowns to help the Buckeyes reach the Rose Bowl. The following season, he ran for 1,450 yards and four scores, and Ohio State advanced to the Rose Bowl again.

THE HEISMAN MEMORIAL TROPHY

.366

CAREER BATTING AVERAGE of Ty Cobb. Playing most of his career with the Detroit Tigers, the Georgia Peach hit over .300 for 23 consecutive seasons and won 12 American League batting titles. Cobb won the AL Triple Crown in 1909 and was the league MVP in 1911. In 1936, he was in the first class of players inducted into the Baseball Hall of Fame.

2,679

MEDALS that the United States has won at the Olympics. No other country has been more decorated at the Games. Forty percent of the medals (1,076) have been gold.

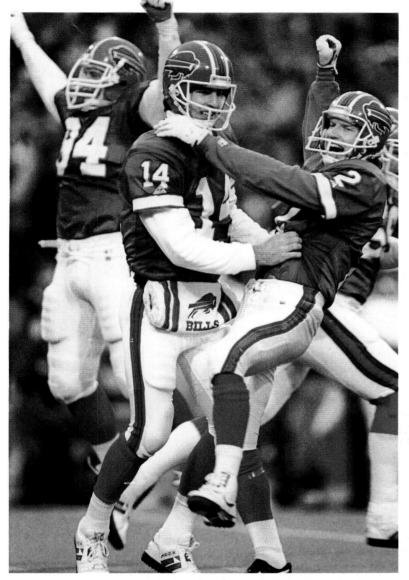

59¹⁄₃

CONSECUTIVE SCORELESS INNINGS thrown by Los Angeles Dodgers pitcher **Orel Hershiser** in 1988. Hershiser surrendered two runs in a game against the Montreal Expos on August 30, then did not allow another run for the rest of the season. His streak lasted six games, all of which he pitched nine innings or more. In the playoffs Hershiser pitched eight scoreless innings in Game 1 of the National League Championship Series before the New York Mets finally got on the board and beat the Dodgers.

32

POINTS by which the **Buffalo Bills** trailed the Houston Oilers in a 1992 wild card playoff game. The Oilers jumped out to a 35–3 lead early in the third quarter before Bills quarterback Frank Reich, who was filling in for injured QB Jim Kelly, threw four touchdown passes and kicker Steve Christie booted a game-winning field goal in overtime to give Buffalo a 41–38 win.

10

SCORE of gymnast **Nadia Comaneci** during the uneven bars portion of the team event at the 1976 Summer Olympics. It was the first time that a gymnast had ever earned a perfect score. The scoreboard was not even equipped to show a result of 10.00, so it read 1.00 instead. The 14-year-old scored six additional perfect 10s and went on to become the youngest Olympian to win a gold medal, with first-place finishes in the all-around, balance beam, and uneven bars.

181

RUSHING YARDS by **Colin Kaepernick** in a 2012 NFC divisional playoff game against the Green Bay Packers. It was the highest single-game rushing total by a QB in the regular season or the playoffs. Kaepernick needed just 16 carries to reach his impressive total, and scored on touchdown runs of 20 and 56 yards. He also threw two TDs in the 49ers' 45–31 win.

TOM BRADY: His Numbers

199

OVERALL PICK that the New England Patriots used to select Brady in the sixth round of the 2000 NFL draft.

5

TIMES that Brady has led the Patriots to the Super Bowl. The team has won the big game three times.

10

AFC EAST DIVISION TITLES that the Patriots have won with Brady at QB.

358

CONSECUTIVE PASS ATTEMPTS that Brady threw without an interception over the course of 2010 and '11.

2

TIMES that Brady has won both the regular-season and Super Bowl MVP awards. He and Joe Montana are the only players to win both awards multiple times.

50

TOUCHDOWN PASSES that Brady threw during the 2010 season to set the single-season record. Twenty-three of those went to Randy Moss, who also set the NFL single-season mark for receiving TDs.

27

WORLD SERIES CHAMPIONSHIPS won by the **New York Yankees**. The Bronx Bombers have been to the Fall Classic 40 times and have taken home the crown 67.5 percent of the time. The team with the second-most World Series titles, the St. Louis Cardinals, has 11.

8

GOLD MEDALS

won by swimmer **Michael Phelps** at the 2008 Beijing Games, the most by an athlete in a single Olympics. He also holds the record for most medals of all time with 22, 18 of which are gold. Phelps, who won his first Olympic medal as a 19-year-old at the 2004 Athens Games, three-peated in the 200-meter individual medley and the 100-meter butterfly, winning the events in 2004, '08, and '12.

18

MAJOR TOURNAMENTS that Jack Nicklaus won. The Golden Bear captured his first major at the 1962 U.S. Open. His last major win was the 1986 Masters, when he was 46 years old. He became the oldest golfer ever to win the event.

5

CONSECUTIVE NASCAR SPRINT CUP SERIES CHAMPIONSHIPS won by **Jimmie Johnson** from 2006 through '10. Johnson started his run by taking the checkered flag at the Daytona 500 in '06 and went on to win his first series title that season. He had won 61 career Sprint Cup races through the 2012 season.

 **SUPER BOWL WINS** by the **Pittsburgh Steelers**. Led by head coach Chuck Noll, the Steelers won the Super Bowl four times in six years during the 1970s. Noll is also the only coach in NFL history to win four Super Bowls. In the early '80s the team adopted the motto "One for the thumb," in reference to its hunt for a fifth ring. After a long drought, Pittsburgh finally got that ring after the 2005 season, and then won its sixth three seasons later.

 **SUPER BOWL LOSSES** by the Buffalo Bills. Their 0–4 record in the big game is the worst in history, and, to make matters worse, the losses all came in a row (Super Bowls XXV, XXVI, XXVII, and XXVIII). Buffalo's best shot was in Super Bowl XXV, when Bills kicker Scott Norwood missed a game-winning field goal and the team lost 20–19 to the New York Giants.

8

CONSECUTIVE NBA CHAMPIONSHIPS won by **Bill Russell**. The Boston Celtics legend won the NBA Finals in 11 of the 13 seasons he was in the league, including eight straight from 1958–59 through 1965–66. Russell was a five-time MVP who was known for his defense. Three times in his career, he finished with 49 or more rebounds in a game.

34.5

POUNDS, weight of the **Stanley Cup**, given to the NHL champion.

30

POUNDS, weight of the **Commissioner's Trophy**, given to the winner of the World Series.

16 POUNDS, weight of the **Larry O'Brien Trophy,** given to the NBA champion.

8 POUNDS, weight of the Waterford crystal **Coaches' Trophy,** given to the BCS college football national champion.

7 POUNDS, weight of the **Vince Lombardi Trophy,** given to the Super Bowl winner.

22

GRAND SLAM SINGLES TITLES

won by **Steffi Graf**, the most in the Open era. What makes Graf's accomplishment even more remarkable is that she dominated at each of the four tournaments. She won the Australian Open four times, the French Open six times, Wimbledon seven times, and the U.S. Open five times. In 1988, she completed the Golden Slam, sweeping the four majors and winning the Olympic gold medal.

17

GRAND SLAM SINGLES TITLES

won by **Roger Federer**, the most by a male tennis player. Federer surpassed Pete Sampras's record at Wimbledon in 2009, the site of seven of Federer's Grand Slam titles. Of his 17, only one has come at the French Open, which he won in 2009.

9

AP NATIONAL CHAMPIONSHIPS won by **Alabama**. The Crimson Tide was tied with Notre Dame going into the 2012 season but grabbed the edge when it defeated the Irish 42–14 in that season's BCS national title game.

MICHAEL JORDAN: HIS NUMBERS

2

OLYMPIC GOLD MEDALS
that Jordan won. He did it once as an amateur, in 1984, and was later part of the first group of NBA players — nicknamed the Dream Team — to compete in the Games in '92.

3

POSITION
where Jordan was selected in the 1984 NBA draft, behind second overall pick Sam Bowie, who never made an All-Star team.

38

NBA GAMES in which Jordan scored at least 50 points.

5

NBA MVP AWARDS
that Jordan won during his career, one behind all-time leader Kareem Abdul-Jabbar.

5.2

SECONDS left when Jordan made his shot over Bryon Russell of the Utah Jazz to clinch the NBA title for the Chicago Bulls in 1998.

72

WINS by the Jordan-led Bulls in 1995–96, the highest single-season win total in NBA history.

6

CHAMPIONSHIPS that Jordan won with the Bulls. The team pulled off two three-peats, one from 1990–91 through '92–93 and another from '95–96 through '97–98.

63

POINTS scored by Jordan in a game against the Boston Celtics in the 1986 playoffs, a postseason record.

32-0

BASKETBALL RECORD of the **Indiana Hoosiers** in 1975–76. Led by coach Bob Knight, the Hoosiers were the last NCAA men's team to go undefeated on its way to the national title. Indiana's streak almost came to an end in the final game of the season. The team trailed Michigan 35–29 at halftime of the championship game but rallied for an 86–68 win.

8

TIMES that sisters **Serena and Venus Williams** have played each other in a Grand Slam final. The first time they squared off in a Grand Slam final was at the 2001 U.S. Open, with Venus winning in straight sets. But that would be one of only two victories that Venus would have over her younger sister, who holds the all-time edge 6–2.

7

CONSECUTIVE MEN'S BASKETBALL NATIONAL CHAMPIONSHIPS that the UCLA Bruins won between 1966–67 and 1972–73. Six other schools plus another UCLA squad are tied for second place, with two. During the Bruins' run, the teams, led by legendary coach **John Wooden** and featuring stars such as Lew Alcindor and Bill Walton, accumulated a record of 205–5.

5

WORLD CUP TITLES won by Brazil, the only country to have qualified for the tournament all 19 times it has been held. Led by soccer legends Pelé, Ronaldo, and Ronaldinho over the years, Brazil won the Cup in 1958, '62, '70, '94, and 2002.

17

TIMES that Jean Beliveau's name was etched on the Stanley Cup. The Montreal Canadiens center led the Habs to 10 titles as a player, with his first coming in 1955–56 and his last in '70–71. After he retired from playing, he remained in the Canadiens' front office as the team went on to win seven more Stanley Cups.

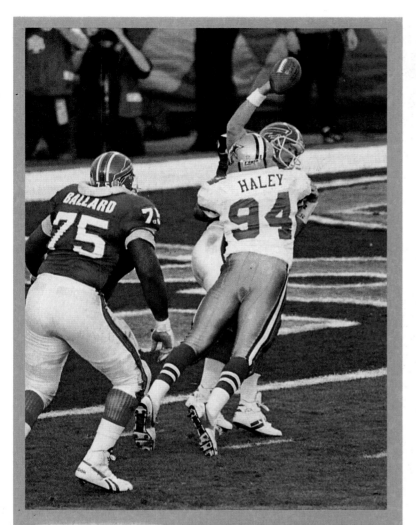

5

SUPER BOWL-WINNING TEAMS that defensive end **Charles Haley** played on. Haley won the Lombardi Trophy twice with the San Francisco 49ers and three times with the Dallas Cowboys. His frequent appearances in the game helped him set the all-time Super Bowl record for sacks with 4.5.

2

TIMES that **Rod Laver** won all four of tennis's Grand Slam tournaments in the same year. Laver captured the men's singles titles at the Australian Open, the French Open, Wimbledon, and the U.S. Open in 1962 and '69. He is the only tennis player to pull off the singles Grand Slam more than once.

20

LEAGUE TITLES that Manchester United has won, the most ever. The Red Devils have also won 11 FA Cups, another record, and secured the UEFA Champions League title three times. In 1998–99, Man U. won the Premier League, FA Cup, and the UEFA Champions League, a feat known as the Treble, with soccer star **David Beckham**.

7

FORMULA 1 DRIVERS' CHAMPIONSHIPS won by **Michael Schumacher**, the most of all time. Widely regarded as the best F1 driver ever, Schumacher won five straight drivers' championships from 2000 to '04. He holds the top two spots in the record book for most wins in a season (13 in 2004 and 11 in '02).

9.58

SECONDS,

time it took Jamaica's Usain Bolt to run 100 meters, a world record. Bolt, the world's fastest man, has set the mark three times.

Here is a history of how the record has progressed since 1960

10.0	ARMIN HARY, *West Germany*	June 21, 1960
9.99	JIM HINES, *United States*	June 20, 1968
9.95	JIM HINES, *United States*	October 14, 1968
9.93	CALVIN SMITH, *United States*	July 3, 1983
9.92	CARL LEWIS, *United States*	September 24, 1988
9.90	LEROY BURRELL, *United States*	June 14, 1991
9.86	CARL LEWIS, *United States*	August 25, 1991
9.85	LEROY BURRELL, *United States*	July 6, 1994
9.84	DONOVAN BAILEY, *Canada*	July 27, 1996
9.79	MAURICE GREENE, *United States*	June 16, 1999
9.77	ASAFA POWELL, *Jamaica*	June 14, 2005
9.74	ASAFA POWELL, *Jamaica*	September 9, 2007
9.72	USAIN BOLT, *Jamaica*	May 31, 2008
9.69	USAIN BOLT, *Jamaica*	August 16, 2008
9.58	USAIN BOLT, *Jamaica*	August 16, 2009

130

STOLEN BASES that Oakland A's speedster **Rickey Henderson** had in 1982, the major league single-season record. Henderson's total was more than all but seven teams' totals in 2012. His record-setting season included two steals of home plate. Henderson is also the major league all-time steals king, with 1,406.

21

SECONDS, time it took right wing **Bill Mosienko** of the Chicago Blackhawks to score a hat trick in a game against the New York Rangers on March 23, 1952. No other NHL player has scored a hat trick faster. In the third period of the regular-season finale, Mosienko pumped three goals past Rangers goalie Lorne Anderson. The Blackhawks were trailing 6–2 at the time, but Mosienko's scores helped propel Chicago to a 7–6 victory.

196.434

MILES PER HOUR, speed of **Danica Patrick**'s qualifying lap at Daytona International Speedway in 2013. Patrick's fast lap helped her become the first woman to win the pole position for the Daytona 500. She finished eighth in the race.

28 YEARS, 17

DAYS,

AGE of LeBron James when he scored his 20,000th NBA point. No other player in the league has reached the milestone faster. The previous record holder was Kobe Bryant, who accomplished it when he was 29 years, 122 days old.

108.8

MILES PER HOUR, speed of Zdeno Chara's slap shot during the 2011–12 NHL All-Star Game Skills Competition. It was the fastest shot ever recorded at the event. The Boston Bruins defenseman shattered his own record in the hardest-shot contest for the third straight year.

0.01

SECONDS, margin of victory for U.S. swimmer **Michael Phelps** over Serbia's Milorad Cavic in the 100-meter butterfly at the 2008 Olympics. Phelps won the race by his fingertips for his seventh gold medal of those Games. He then added one more to break Mark Spitz's record for most golds won at a single Olympics.

105.1

MILES PER HOUR, speed of Cincinnati Reds pitcher **Aroldis Chapman's** fastball during a game against the San Diego Padres in 2010. It was the fastest pitch ever recorded with the Pitch f/x system. All 25 pitches that Chapman threw to the Padres were 100 miles per hour or faster.

11

HORSES that have won the thoroughbred racing Triple Crown. The last horse to do so was Affirmed in 1978, but no horse was more dominant than **Secretariat** in 1973. The chestnut colt set records in the Kentucky Derby, the Preakness Stakes, and the Belmont Stakes, all of which still stand today.

296

RUSHING YARDS by the Minnesota Vikings' **Adrian Peterson** in a 2007 game against the San Diego Chargers. He set the NFL single-game rushing record in only the eighth game of his rookie season. And it wasn't even the first 200-plus-yard rushing game of his career. He ran for 224 yards in his fifth game, against the Chicago Bears. Peterson went on to win the Offensive Rookie of the Year Award. He was the NFL MVP in 2012 after coming just eight yards short of setting the single-season rushing record with 2,097 yards.

163.4

MILES PER HOUR, speed of a serve by Australian **Samuel Groth** at the 2012 Busan Open. It is the fastest serve ever clocked at a professional tennis event. Groth had two other serves reach 157.5 and 158.9 miles per hour, respectively. Despite his speedy slams, Groth still lost the match to Uladzimir Ignatik.

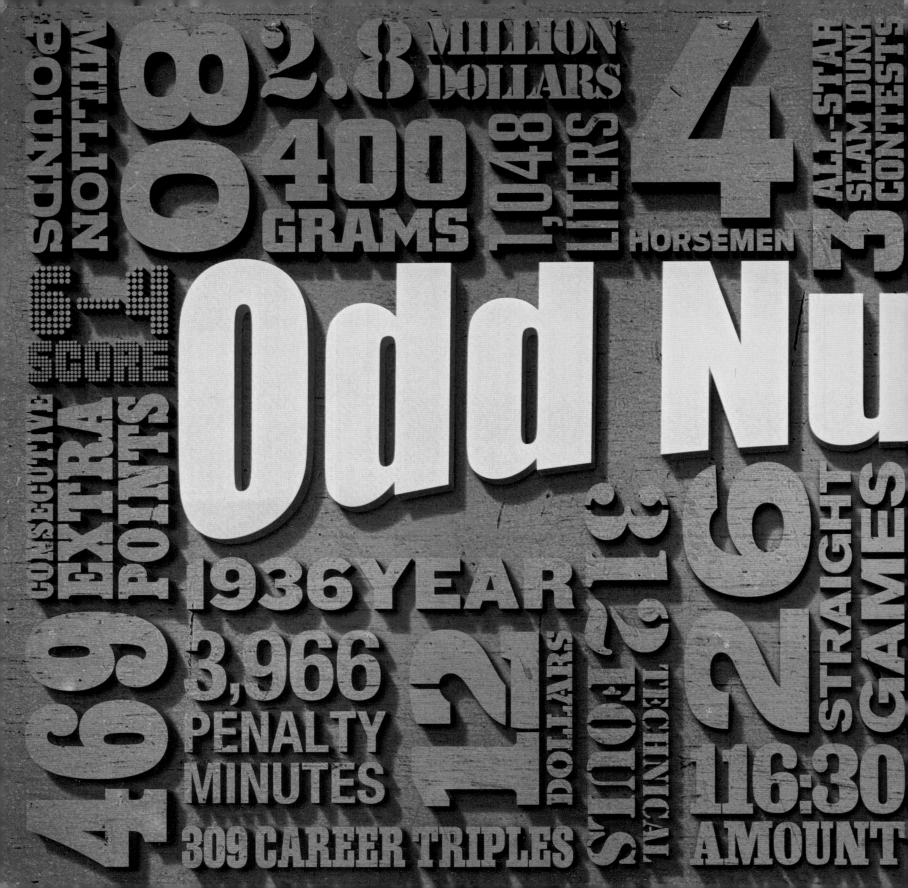

2

CONSECUTIVE HOME RUNS

hit by players named Ken Griffey. On September 14, 1990, the Seattle Mariners' Ken Griffey Sr. went yard against California Angels pitcher Kirk McCaskill. The next batter was Griffey's son **Ken Griffey Jr.** He hit a homer as well, making the Griffeys the first father-son duo to hit back-to-back home runs in the big leagues.

26

STRAIGHT GAMES that the Tampa Bay Buccaneers lost, the longest streak in NFL history. The Bucs did not make a good first impression when they joined the league in 1976, losing all 14 of their games that season. They did not make the best second impression either, losing their first 12 contests in 1977. Tampa Bay finally got its first win on December 11, 1977, against the New Orleans Saints.

52

YEARS OLD, age of **Gordie Howe** when he became the oldest player to compete in an NHL game, in 1980. Mr. Hockey appeared in 80 games for the Hartford Whalers during the 1979–80 season, playing alongside two of his sons, Mark and Marty. In 1997, he suited up for the Detroit Vipers of the IHL for one shift at the age of 69, becoming the first person to play professional hockey in six decades (1940s through '90s).

312

TECHNICAL FOULS assessed to Rasheed Wallace in his NBA career. Wallace has been T'd up at least 17 times in 11 of his 16 NBA seasons. He set the single-season mark for technicals in 2000–01, with 40.

3,966

PENALTY MINUTES by Dave (Tiger) Williams. No other NHL player has spent more time in the penalty box. That's the equivalent of more than 66 entire games. Williams led the league in penalty minutes three times and spent an average of 4.12 minutes per game in the box.

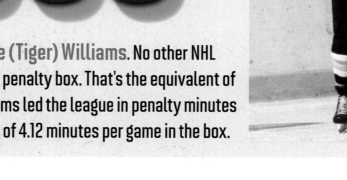

109,901

SEATING CAPACITY of **Michigan Stadium**, home of the University of Michigan Wolverines football team. Nicknamed the Big House, it is the largest stadium in the country. Every home game since November 8, 1975, has drawn a crowd of at least 100,000 fans.

BACKFLIPS in one jump that Travis Pastrana pulled off during the Moto X Best Trick event at the 2006 X Games. Pastrana was the first rider to successfully complete the trick in competition.

25

ALL-STAR GAMES that Hank Aaron played in. Aaron was chosen to play in the Midsummer Classic in 21 of the 23 seasons that he played with the Milwaukee Braves, Atlanta Braves, and Milwaukee Brewers. (The only two seasons he missed were his first, 1954, and his last, 1976.) His remarkable stat was helped by the fact that Major League Baseball held two All-Star Games from 1959 through '62.

12

DOLLARS, cost of the most expensive ticket to Super Bowl I, between the Green Bay Packers and the Kansas City Chiefs. At Super Bowl XLVII, between the Baltimore Ravens and the San Francisco 49ers, the face value of the most expensive ticket was $1,200.

7'7"

HEIGHT of Gheorghe Muresan, the tallest player in NBA history. The center from Romania played six seasons in the league with the Washington Bullets and New Jersey Nets. Muresan also appeared in the 1998 movie *My Giant*.

5'3"

HEIGHT of Muggsy Bogues, the shortest player in NBA history. Bogues played for 14 seasons with four teams. The speedy guard finished in the top 10 in assists six times and blocked 39 shots during his career, despite his short stature.

10

NHL GOALIES who have scored a goal. The netminder to do so most recently was **Martin Brodeur** of the New Jersey Devils, who shot a puck into an empty net on March 21, 2013, against the Carolina Hurricanes. It was the third goal of Brodeur's career. No other goalie has scored more times.

3

ALL-STAR SLAM DUNK CONTESTS won by **Nate Robinson**. The 5'9" guard was crowned champion for the first time in 2005–06 and won back-to-back titles in '08–09 and '09–10. One of his dunk-contest-winning moves involved skying over 6'11" Dwight Howard before throwing down a slam.

147,500,000,000,000,000,000

POSSIBLE WAYS to fill out a 68-team **NCAA men's basketball tournament** bracket, according to DePaul University math professor Jeffrey Burgan. In case you lost count of the zeroes, this figure is read as 147.5 quintillion!

First draft of Basket Ball rules.
thing in the gym that the boys might learn the rules— Dec. 1891 James Naismith
6-28-31.

13

RULES that Dr. James Naismith wrote down when he created the new game of Basket Ball at the Springfield (Massachusetts) YMCA in 1891. In basketball's original rules, a game consisted of only two 15-minute halves, and if a team committed three consecutive fouls, its opponent would be awarded a goal.

50

TIMES that Montreal Expos infielder **Ron Hunt** was hit by a pitch in 1971, a single-season record. Hunt led the National League in beanings for seven straight seasons from 1968 through '74 and finished his career having been plunked 243 times.

3

FREE THROWS

that Loyola Marymount guard **Bo Kimble** shot with his left hand in the 1990 NCAA men's basketball tournament. The righthanded Kimble wore a 44 patch and used his left hand in honor of his late teammate Hank Gathers, who took free throws lefthanded.

SCORE of the first intercollegiate football game, in which **Rutgers College** beat the **College of New Jersey** (now Princeton), in 1869. Each team had 25 men on the field, and players could advance the ball only by kicking or batting it with their head, feet, hands, or sides of their body.

309

CAREER TRIPLES by **Sam Crawford** during his 19 seasons with the Cincinnati Reds and Detroit Tigers. Crawford led the National League in three-baggers once and the American League five times, including three seasons in a row (1913 to '15). Crawford finished with fewer than 10 triples only twice in his career, his first season and his last.

80

MILLION POUNDS, amount that Real Madrid paid Manchester United for **Cristiano Ronaldo**. It is the highest transfer fee ever paid for a soccer player. Ronaldo has led Real Madrid to Copa Del Rey and La Liga titles and was the first player in a top European league to score at least 40 goals in back-to-back seasons.

1,048

LITERS of water that a **Zamboni 560AC** model ice resurfacing machine can hold.

1936

YEAR that Louis Meyer drank a glass of buttermilk after winning the Indianapolis 500, starting a tradition that has carried on every year except from 1947 through '55. Today, winners like three-time champion **Dario Franchitti** quench their thirst with regular milk.

35

COLLEGE FOOTBALL BOWL GAMES that will be played in the 2013–14 season. In 1902, the **Rose Bowl** was the first and only bowl game played. The number of Bowl games did not reach double digits until 1946.

469

CONSECUTIVE EXTRA POINTS

kicked through the uprights by **Matt Stover**. Stover's streak started in 1996, and he maintained it through the duration of his NFL career, which ended in 2009.

28

HOME RUNS that **Josh Hamilton** of the Texas Rangers hit in the first round of the 2008 Home Run Derby. Hamilton set the single-round record for homers in the derby. His longest shot traveled an estimated 518 feet. Despite his first-round score, Hamilton lost in the final to the Minnesota Twins' Justin Morneau.

116:30

AMOUNT of overtime played in a 1936 playoff game between the Detroit Red Wings and the Montreal Maroons. Detroit's Mud Bruneteau scored in the sixth overtime period to give the Wings a 1–0 victory.

370

TOTAL POINTS scored in a game between the Denver Nuggets and the Detroit Pistons on December 13, 1983. It was the highest combined score in NBA history, with the Pistons winning 186–184 in triple overtime. Twelve players scored in double figures, including Denver's **Dan Issel**, who finished with 28 points. Nuggets forward Kiki Vandeweghe led all scorers with 51 points.

4

HORSEMEN, nickname given to Notre Dame's backfield of Don Miller, Elmer Layden, Jim Crowley, and Harry Stuhldreher after the Fighting Irish defeated Army 13–7 in 1924. Acclaimed sportswriter Grantland Rice coined the term in his story for the *New York Herald Tribune* after the game.

PITTSBURG

WAGNER, PITTSBURG

2.8

MILLION DOLLARS, amount paid for a 1909 T206 **Honus Wagner baseball card** by Arizona Diamondbacks owner Ken Kendrick in 2007. It is the most valuable baseball card in history.

400

GRAMS, weight of an **Olympic gold medal** from the 2012 Summer Games in London. Olympic gold medals are actually made mostly of silver, but must contain at least six grams of real gold.

INDEX

INDEX

GOLF

HOCKEY

HORSE RACING

MOTOR SPORTS

OLYMPIC SPORTS

SOCCER

SURFING

TENNIS

X GAMES

PHOTO CREDITS